Childhood Trauma Pursuing Real Estate

Childhood Trauma Pursuing Real Estate

Livia Worley

To order additional copies of this book, contact:
Xlibris
1-888-795-4274
www.Xlibris.com
Orders@Xlibris.com
814031

CONTENTS

GOOD OL' CHILDHOOD

I WAS VERY poor growing up. Very poor. I remember having $10 to buy my school shoes at the beginning of the year that I would wear the entire school year. At least I had shoes. I was brought into this world having one sister, one bother, and two parents. Like many, we moved a lot when I was young. My bio parents lived together until I was about five years old. I'm twenty-seven years old, but I remember the last year of them like they happened yesterday. I watched someone who was angry all the time. I watched them get to the point they physically abused another in front of me until there was blood everywhere, and they were crying for help. My sister and I were so scared one night we ran to the next-door neighbor's house barefoot in the middle of the night for help. Much more I'd rather not discuss, but it was rough.

I didn't know the disease alcoholism and how it affects someone's life. I didn't know at the time that was the result of too many drinks. I was just a child. I watched someone struggle with mental health issues that I also couldn't recognize as a child. Every decision didn't have a logical reason behind it. They were also really angry beyond recognition at times and overly filled with joy at other times.

We were removed from our home by CPS. Allegations of child abuse and neglect had been reported. Two of us went to live with my granny for a couple of years. I also watched someone close to me in a separate incident go to prison for twenty years. They were there one day and gone the next. Just a rough start for a five-year-old in the real world.

My dreams about my future success were like most six-year olds at that time. I wanted to be a schoolteacher. More than I wanted to be a schoolteacher, I wanted money. I dreamed about having things other kids had. Now that I think about it, I probably wanted to partly be a teacher because they were safe and nice to me without knowing exactly what my life was like after school hours.

Living with my grandma gave me the stability I desperately needed at six years old. She gave us daily structure we didn't have. She lived on land that belonged to her daughter, my aunt. I had a couple of cousins who lived next door to my grandma.

It was my first REAL experience around money. It gave me my first thoughts of what money even is and what people value things at and what money can do for someone. They lived in a huge beautiful two-story home with a huge red barn and a dog kennel that housed about six dogs at a time. My cousin's dad wore many hats. He was a breeder of K9 German shepherds. He bred, raised, and trained them for the police academy. He also worked many years as a chemist/chemical engineer for creditable companies like a local one in Michigan, Upjohn Pharmaceutical Company. My cousin's mother had multiple flows of income as well. She worked for the local county as a worker who managed welfare coverage in the community. She also was an Avon rep, back when they made decent money. It was a complete change in environment, a bit of a culture shock to a small child.

I didn't see my bio mother or father during the time we stayed with my grandma. No one explained to us at the time what was going on. They don't explain these types of things to children. Parents and adults don't explain much of anything to kids. I'm not sure that was the best decision. I thought no one wanted us anymore. I grew super close to my grandma and loved being there. My bio mother had to prove to the court she could take care of us financially, physically, and emotionally.

After a few years, my bio mother came back around and was able to legally have us back from our grandma. That was tough because I no longer wanted to be with her. I knew it was an environment I didn't want to go back to. I also became super attached to my grandma. There wasn't anyone angry there. We got to eat cereal at night, play outside on a swing set most days, eat hot breakfast before school, and have money when this "tooth fairy" came through. I grew attached to my granny.

Even worse, I went to live back with my bio mom and her new husband at the age of eight, and my granny passed away two years later, two days after my tenth birthday. Even though it's been seventeen years and I was young, it has had a lifelong impact on me. I think about her all the time. I think about what she would be like now. How proud would she be? What would our relationship look like? I miss all her cooking. She was full-blooded Mexican and could cook REAL good. I remember that most about her and watching her soaps.

My bio mom brought a new man with her. I didn't know at the time that that man would be the person to mold me into the person I am today and teach me so many life lessons. I grew close to him over the years. He taught me the difference between street-smart and book smart. He taught me the importance of making the right decision that will benefit not only me but also the people around me. I learned what rational thinking versus irrational thinking was, not how a traditional parent would teach it. Traditional parents talk their children to death. This man showed me how to be a good person with actions not his words. I just chose to take a harder route in this life.

You may be wondering where my bio dad is and what happened to him. Well, my sister and I saw him a couple of times for maybe an overnight camping or canoe trip. My mother would assure us if we just called and left a message, he would call us back. He never did. I just heard a lot of "You've reached the voicemail box of . . ." When we needed school clothes, it seemed she hoped he picked up as much as we did.

Living with her new husband, we didn't live much better than before, but at least this man didn't seem to ever get angry. Even when there were times to be angry, he never seemed it. We went right back to living poorly, never having money for anything, barely for what we needed. If we didn't have it for what we needed, we went without.

Since I had those few years with my granny and saw what money could do, I always knew I wanted some. I just didn't understand how to get it. No one tells children how adults make money. No one told us how my aunt and uncle made their money. No one told us if they were even doing it right and if it could be done better than them.

MENTAL HEALTH AND ALCOHOLISM

P EOPLE HAVE DIFFERENT thoughts come to mind when they hear or read mental health. Mental health issues can be severe, light, or moderate in appearance. Some people overcome the trauma they endured in life well, and some don't. Some people end up angry adults who abuse drugs and alcohol. Those same adults have kids. This is the sad reality many kids are born into. Some of it is genetic and some of it gained from the environment in which we grow up. Drug abuse and alcoholism doesn't just take over one life; it takes over the whole household. It has a ripple effect on the whole family. These are serious harsh realities. I encourage finding support and help.

I wanted to break the cycle. I didn't want to pass some of the same traumas I endured as a child to my son. Now I know I can't protect him from everything, and he will have his own issues to deal with because we all do. I hope to limit his exposure to some of the more serious childhood traumas that impact lots of adults today.

GOOD OL' SCHOOL DAYS

MOST SCHOOL YEARS, I was picked on for what I wore and how I looked. I took a bath every day, but the kids always still seemed to call me dirty. The school bus has some of the worst memories for most kids. Lots of older kids tend to target the younger kids. Like most kids who came from the same struggle as me, I found I had to be a certain way, the only way I knew how to be to survive. I had to be tough. I had to fight. It was through fighting that I gained respect and "friends." The more people I stood up to, the fewer kids who wanted to pick on me and more kids who wanted to be my friend. I grew more rebellious as years went on. I thought I found a better, stronger way of living my life. My friends list did grow longer. They weren't the best kids to be friends with, but at least they were forced to be kind, and I wasn't going to let them pick on me.

I had an older friend who had an aunt I claimed as my own. We loved hanging out with her. We were always at her house on the weekends. She took us everywhere and even got us into a local club for twenty-one-year-olds and older. Here was where I saw a lot of cash on one person. One night while we were out late, I saw a man who had tons of cash in his pocket. I didn't know what he did to get the money, but I had a feeling at fifteen that it wasn't legal. As I walked by him, my aunt said, "DAMN, that's a lot of money!" He replied, "Yeah, and I'm good at it too."

My first money light bulb went off. What am I good at?

Around this time, I saw my first pound of weed. It was bought and then divided into quarter pounds, and then into ounces, and then into quarters. They gave me some to try and start selling to all my friends who either smoked or knew someone older who did. It worked. It worked well. Again, since there was no one to teach me the ropes, I learned on my own. Fast money comes greed. I wanted more than what the weed selling could do. I organized a group of girls from my school to start stealing big ticket items to resell later.

You might wonder where my guidance through these nights was. Well, my bio mom didn't give my new dad any control in the household. He knew I was out living my best life. His only advice was to be smart about it, trust no one, and don't ever let anyone hit you first. My bio mom always tried to stop me from hanging out with the friends she thought were bad. She had bad judgment. She stopped me from hanging out with good friends all the time because she thought they were bad. In return, I could hang out with the ones who weren't necessarily bad, but we had more opportunities to get into trouble. Anything she tried to tell me after that didn't hold much substance. I felt abandoned as a child, left unprotected, and lied to and felt I was showed how a mother was not supposed to be.

Just like most young people, I had the right idea. I was just channeling it all the wrong ways. I didn't have anyone around me teaching me about money. No one talks to young people about money. Everyone always wants to talk about someone's "bad" decisions. Adults always tell young people where they could end up when they continue to make bad decisions, but no one talks about where a child could end up if they had made all the right decisions. Or how someone can make all the right decisions and still end up with the short end of the stick. I grew further apart from adults and what they had to say.

GOOD OL' COURT SYSTEM

M Y MOTHER THOUGHT I was becoming so reckless; she would call the cops on me when I left the house or chose to sneak and hang out with the friends she didn't approve of. Here, I was like so many what society has deemed "troubled youth." I was in and out of juvenile because cops were called almost every time a situation at home happened. No one cared enough to figure out what traumas I might have endured and how I might be triggered at times to respond a certain way. What my bio mom didn't tell them was my childhood. I was so angry with her. We never seemed to agree on anything. I always felt she told the court what she wanted them to hear, only the things she wanted me to work on. How can a child work on themselves if they have to worry about taking care of everything? What my bio mom didn't tell them was that she thought the best option for our family was for her two daughters to pay rent to stay with her at sixteen years old. What she didn't tell them was the money I was making away from home was paying for rides for my new dad to get to and from work while she took their only car out to hang with her own friends. She didn't tell them the countless arguments we had where she lost control. I had to be an adult before I should've been. The court treated me like the child who I wasn't.

By this time, the court system tried to reprehend me to the house via house arrest. I had another older friend whose parents wanted her to find honest work. It was through this friend that I was able to get permission from my probation officer to work while on tether. She found us both a job working seven days a week for seven hours a day, paid cash at the end of each day. Couldn't beat it! A young teenager to be making $250 a week in 2007–2008 was a big deal. You would hope that it was enough to get me back on track and to stay in school. There is only one flaw to this thought process.

I didn't change my way of thinking about money, I didn't change my bad habits, I didn't change those kids I surrounded myself with, and last, I did not have a mentor, someone to look up to about money. The court gave me so many opportunities to straighten it out. I thought I couldn't spend more than a couple of weeks in juvenile, so I thought.

The last straw for the court was me cutting my tether. I was on tether and my bio mom was out with her friends when I decided to invite a few people over to drink and hang out. One kid got too drunk, so we put him out. We thought, well, if you can't handle drinking, you shouldn't be here, and you should go. Well, he ended up in the parking lot of the apartment complex passed out, drunk in his car. Long story short, the police eventually was called, and the kid told them where they were drinking. I ended up catching a MIPI (minor in possession of intoxication). After the police left and I had a ticket in my hand and court in four days, I decided my best exit route was to cut my tether. I spent three months in a local juvenile court in Michigan. After three months in juvenile, my probation officer informed me I was going to be moved to a residential facility for juveniles. In other words, I better sit tight because I'm going to be locked up for a while. I knew that, and I still cried. All I thought about was my friends and family. I wondered how long I was really going to be gone for. I didn't know at the time it was going to be over a year before they let me return to society.

In that year, there were a lot of money and resources spent to keep me in that place that could've been saved. I can't say today I came out of there with practical skills or toolbox of goodies. I walked out knowing I never wanted to come back. It was a lived experience you can't get anywhere else. There were kids there who inspired me to be grateful. There were staff there whom I didn't like, and there were ones I did like. There was only one counselor who truly made an impact on me, good or bad. I started at this residential facility pissed off half the time. I walked around angry. I didn't want to talk to anyone, kids or adults. I didn't care for anyone there. I thought, how could anyone possibly know anything about what I've been through? Yet there was one sentence that he said that changed my whole approach to getting out of there. He asked me one day, "Why don't you at least fake it till you make it?"

He didn't understand why I wasn't trying to pull a fast one and act like I'm making better decisions. He was wondering why I wasn't even trying to pull one over just so I could go home. He knew I was smart but not smart enough to figure that much out. What he didn't know at the time was that I couldn't and didn't have anything to care for, even myself. Again, another light bulb went off. Could I fake it until I make it? So from then on, I "faked" being well behaved. I started following instructions and jumping in to help wherever I could. This was one of those many moments that changed my way of thinking.

As I sat in locked up and things got a little easier and adults began to trust me a little more, I was called to the front desk area, where staff usually talk to kids and give them any important updates. I had been doing better, so I didn't think it was bad. As I walked to the front desk, I had this uneasy feeling. The staff member shut the door behind me. My bio mom called and left a message. It was the moment I had to hear another person close to me went to jail. She didn't want to talk to me, or she couldn't. I'm not sure. It began to sit in, disappointment. I thought how sad that must be for my bio mom. I didn't want to be a part of that circle anymore. I didn't want to disappoint anyone close to me anymore. I couldn't be there for anyone, even myself. Being in residential makes you forget about what's going on in the real world and how helpless you are to those who may need you.

While I was locked up, I couldn't get out even after all the effort I put forward to do well. We didn't meet one of the conditions of the court—a safe and established place of residence. I was the only one of the kids underage whom the court felt still needed to be under certain living conditions based on age. My bio mom and new dad moved to a new city and landed a new house to rent after about six months.

FINALLY, I WAS able to come home. Unfortunately, it was all the same environment. After making it off probation, I dropped out of high school. I found out I was five weeks pregnant at the age of seventeen. I knew it wasn't going to be just me anymore. How would my unborn child and I going to survive? I found out about a program in the community that helps with education and work. I was able to achieve employment that hired felons and obtain my GED certification before my son was born. I grew super close to the owner of the business I worked for. He knew my struggles with my mother. He owned properties and offered for me to live there until I got my own place. I took his offer and continued my education. I continued in achieving my associate degree in business administration going part time while having my son. I continued to work there for five more years, yet I knew I still wanted more. I had made it this far in life because of those people who gave me a chance with employment. It was a chocolate shop that solely hires kids with charges from the juvenile system. The owner was also the first person to introduce me to real estate, landlord–tenant contracts, and rental properties. He is also a state licensed builder. I didn't think at that time that I would go that route or how much I would love real estate.

After five years of working there, it was through that owner that I was able to obtain a higher-paying job, and still to this day, I stay in close contact with him. I have him look at all my properties before buying, ensuring a good buy. He is also one of the first people to introduce me to real estate. It's important to me to have loyal, trustworthy people as part of my business.

That chocolate shop was my stable foundation to rebuilding my life. I came to them dirt poor, no education, and pregnant. The owner and his mother were exactly what I needed. They were kind. They were supportive. A lot of people struggle with day jobs because their homelife is a mess. They were up late because they had a baby up late or arguing with family members about contributing more. Maybe their car broke down in the morning, and that was their only transportation. Maybe they had to spend their only gas money to get to work on their baby who needed formula. This owner understood the struggle and took every chance he could to understand circumstances and to help support kids going through them.

Now I spend my time at the chocolate shop much differently. I go there to visit and share how I'm doing. I go there to get caught up on what's going on in their lives. I speak with new employees to help inspire them to keep coming and to build a future for themselves that they would be proud of. His shop's mission is what other businesses wouldn't prefer. He wanted young people who have been involved with the courts and struggled to overcome and obtain basic needs. He wants and continues to give young people a foundation to build off. He and his family want people to succeed. They are just genuinely good people, once-in-your-lifetime type of people.

I was just there speaking with a young lady who works there who is struggling with addiction and wants to drop out of school. School is not for everyone, but if it's not for you, you need to know what you want to create and sell. She was interested in real estate. She heard I was in it. We exchanged numbers. I applaud her. Build relationships with people who are doing what you want to do. If it is real estate, hang with investors, bankers, lenders, realtors, etc. You never know who people are and what they have to offer the world with their talents. I told her she can call me anytime she wants to talk about beginning a real estate journey. That's a small way I give back to the very people who put me in a position to succeed as they are now doing with this young lady.

HAVING A CHILD AT EIGHTEEN YEARS OLD

I FOUND OUT I was five weeks pregnant at the age of seventeen. I was put out of my bio mother's house a few weeks after that. As you heard, we never could see eye to eye and wasn't going to start with that news. Being locked up for over a year had its impact but nothing like knowing you are bringing a life into this world and asking yourself, what do you have to offer that life?

I didn't have anything. I was living with my mother on the verge of being put out, dropped out of high school as soon as I got off probation, and had no job and wasn't even looking for one. What was I going to do?

I was venting to a friend who had lived in the area longer. She told me about the program that changed my route in life—YOU. It's a program that helps kids between the ages of sixteen and twenty-four, at the time, obtain employment and help them get back into school and obtain either their high school diploma or GED.

If I didn't find out I was pregnant at that moment, who knows where I would be now? Many people look at their kids as setbacks and use them as excuses not to do things. I use our son as motivation—motivation to build something and have something to offer this new life I brought into this world. A parent naturally wants to give their child everything in the world. I use that bond to build on the dreams I have for my family.

Our son is singlehandedly the biggest motivation in my life. I hear parents all the time say their children is why they can't do something; it reminds me of how extremely important it is to have the right mind-set about things and about any situation you are in. It will determine your success. I don't understand those who have kids and don't want to give them the world or make it seem like we can only give our kids love or the world and not both. I don't understand those people. Our son will have both.

WHAT HELD ME BACK?

ANYONE WHO HAS been through something in their life responds in a certain way after they go through it. Mine was anger. I responded with anger in every situation I ended up in. I was angry growing up. I didn't understand why I was going through all this. Why did I have to grow up having nothing, watching my parents fight, splitting up from my siblings, coming back together to watch it all over again? I blamed my parents for how I felt. It left me with very little positive feelings. I had to want something different. I had to stop the poor-me attitude, the thought that no one knows what it's like to be me. I didn't trust anyone growing up, and it cost me everything. I missed opportunities because I didn't care enough and felt I could do everything on my own.

It wasn't until I realized I was the one holding me back before I made a real change. Before I got to see real progress, I had to understand it was changes I had to make to get me there, not anyone else's choices. I also had to face failure, but it starts with how we view the world and the circumstances we can't control. I fear our son will be taught to know right from wrong and how things he chooses to do have a direct effect on what comes his way. How do you prepare someone to understand you can do everything right and still lose and it's still okay? You can do all the right planning and preparing and still fail at accomplishing it.

Growing up, I thought the world was against me, and somehow again, I got the short end of the stick. Now I choose to find a way to either figure it out and overcome it or switch my focus to something I can accomplish. Maybe I find someone to help and partner up. Well then, again, the way you treat people matters. Again, growing up, no professional would want to partner with me being a ticking time bomb at any moment. Why would they risk everything for someone who could help them lose it all? These are the very things that held me back growing up from really accomplishing something. Who knows? Maybe I would've finished high school and started investing earlier. I hope someone reading this doesn't hold themselves back any longer.

YOU PROGRAM

I STAY IN contact with all those people and programs that have touched my life. Five years after the YOU community resource helped me obtain employment and my GED certification while six months pregnant, they also approved me to come back and volunteer with other young people coming to the program. They are trying to create something for themselves on their own. Just like some of you who bought this book, these kids want and are willing to work for something better in their lives. Kids must be self-disciplined and self-motivated to successfully complete this community resource. These kids aren't forced to be here by their parents or the court. These kids don't have anyone waking them up and telling them to dress for the day. These kids do it themselves. Some with their own kids on the way or already here. As a person who wants to be successful, you must have what these kids have. You must be able to get up in the morning before your alarm goes off. You should be starting the solution before the problem arises. Just call it preventative services, preventing yourself from going broke. You must want it more than the person next to you.

I love that type of audience, makes my job easier. I don't have to beg them to do something for themselves. They don't give you a million reasons why they can't do it or even show up. They come. They're hungry. I mean it. They can't just be present and think that's enough. They must be starving when they show up. That is something that comes from within yourself. If you have a seed, water it. Give it resources to grow. I love getting people excited about their future. Everyone who wants success and works for it deserves it. It does not come overnight. I'm twenty-seven and have been working at this since I was eighteen. It doesn't happen overnight, and it isn't one big step to success. It's millions of little steps. It only starts with a step like I took with YOU.

THE REAL ESTATE START

I MET MY fiancé in 2012. He really liked real estate. I watched him put countless hours into studying material, deal searching, stacking money for a down payment. I watched him get a couple of properties, even put up my money to help get some before I really started to see his results. I wasn't doing anything with my money like that at all. By the time he was buying his tenth house, I began to save. I knew it didn't take that much money to get started in our local real estate market. You must know the numbers for your local market to understand how much you need to get started.

My plan was to save enough until I had enough to invest to make me more. Once I had about $10,000 saved, I went to the bank to see if they would consider buying the real estate for me, and I could make the down payment and every mortgage payment after purchase. You can buy a house out right with cash, but if you don't have much funds to start with like me, you probably won't start there. I used the bank's money instead of using my own. I used their money to invest in an income-producing rental property. I created cash flow by putting a tenant in the house to pay down the debt. You grow these kinds of investments by your money management skills. You can take the rent money from the tenant and go spend every dollar, but don't expect to keep your investment for very long.

Same concept if someone gets a raise from working their day job. A worker with a raise will feel as if they have more money to spend. They never think about that raise being something they can save. If you spend every dollar that you make, you will not last in much related to investing and business. If you want to make money, you put tons of research and planning after finding something someone is already doing that is making money. You master it. People build a brand off themselves and then create a clothing line brand and become rich. People buy houses to rent out or to rehab and flip already. I'm not the first, and I won't be the last. Everything surrounding our every day lives is someone else's source of income. We just don't ever think about it. We are in what experts call the overloading of information. Give someone too much information at once and they cannot process it all.

MONEY THAT WE DON'T TALK ABOUT

THERE'S SO MUCH around us that no one ever talks about it. My bio mom and new dad never talked about money unless it was about how they didn't have it. There was never enough was all I knew as a child. My bio mom worked hard to provide the little we had, harder than I wanted her to. She worked three jobs to make ends meet and so my sister and I could have a couple of family vacations. Christmas we usually spent at a local church, getting things we needed for winter—coats, boots, scarf, and if we're lucky, a board game to take home. At the time, you don't understand being grateful. You wonder why everyone else gets everything you want. My bio mom had the right idea about more money, but she applied it all wrong. Instead of creating value that someone else will buy, she worked harder and asked for more hours, a way to take care of her family but not a way to get rich. She couldn't help it much. She came from a very poor family, and they took pride in working hard, long days. Parents don't see their influence as negative. How could that be? What most parents don't understand is the world is changing, and that's now how our kids will be raised to think. They are exposed to ways more than our grandparents could've imagined at that age. You end up stunting your family's growth with this thought process. I say this from experience. I watched my mom work as hard as anyone else, yet my imagination only went as for as my bio mom. I thought as a little girl I could work three jobs too. Not once as a kid did I think I could not work at all and make millions. I dreamed of having a lot of money, but I just thought I had to either get lucky and hit the lotto or be born into a rich family or something. Maybe even go off and play in the WNBA.

THE BASICS OF PARENTING
THROUGH MY EXPERIENCE

P ARENTS HAVE BEEN struggling since the beginning of time to get along with their kids, understand what their kids like and don't like, or even coexist in the same household. So many parents don't understand why their kids make some of the decisions they make. They're always looking at what's wrong with their child instead of what happened to them. Kids experience things that adults don't notice they fail at acknowledging or are blinded by their own child's innocence and can't see what their child is experiencing. They don't see kids as worriers or overthinkers. What may be going on in the home affecting the child? Any recent breakups? Any domestic violence in the house? Did someone hurt them? At home or at school? These are very serious, life-altering things that parents don't take in consideration in a heated moment because either they weren't directly involved or they don't know about it. It's these kinds of experiences that shape our kids. These kids grow up to be working professionals of society if they're lucky enough. Young people who grew up like me don't have people around them who spoke to them about these things. Maybe adults think kids are too young to feel the impact of what is going on around them. I watched someone close to me go to prison for a twenty-year sentence by the time I turned six years old. No one ever talked to me about this. Instead, adults let years of that kid's life go by and decide when they saw behavior they didn't like, they tried to forcibly change it. Understanding the root or the cause will help parents approach their kids in a healthy, more helpful way. How can a kid possibly think about future success when they're always worried about what's happening or what's going to happen? Help relieve them of that burden, and it could help make a difference in the relationship and how much focus they can put on their future.

MENTALITY CHECK

ONE MORNING, I was getting dressed for work when I heard "BOOOOOM!" I hurried to my window to look out the curtain to find out my Chevy Trailblazer had been completely smashed in the back. I was so upset and helpless. Here is a mentality check. I had to go get an estimate for the insurance company. My estimate was for $5,200. I had three different people tell me to do the exact same thing with the $5,200. They wanted me to take my $5,200 and use it for a down payment on a new car. The Trailblazer that had been smashed was completely paid off. I used it to get to work every day, and that's it. My mind told me to find some way to take advantage of the situation and find an opportunity out of this stressful incident. Maybe find a way to spend some and save the rest for another down payment on a house that could produce me another income instead of what everyone else was telling me. Throw more money out the window! Take on a monthly payment to a new car! Give myself another bill I can't keep up with! Use the tough time to stress spend! They were trying to satisfy their instant gratification or what some people will disguise as "positive thinking." Don't fall for "positive thinking" that isn't money smart. I'll tell you what, that's the fastest way your bank account will stay at zero.

STICKING WITH IT

S O MANY OF us kids growing up have plenty of ideas they bring to their parents; so many parents either dismiss or redirect the conversation to what their kid "needs" to do. Parents can help kids plan out these ideas and follow through. It doesn't matter how big or small the idea. We as kids won't stick with it if we don't have encouragement and a structured process to follow. Structure a process for a kid to follow. Think about a process for a lemonade stand, simple enough for an eight-year-old. The following are the materials needed and the cost of those materials:

Signs – $5
Table – $20
Tablecloth – $5
Chair – $5
Cups – $5
Pitcher – $1
Kool-Aid – $5
Sugar – $5
Change drawer to start – $10

Ask them how they will buy these materials. The whole concept of my book is overcoming trauma and saving your money to invest. Give them options and ideas. Doing dishes, sweeping, mopping, cleaning their room, taking out trash, reading, anything to save enough money to buy all the materials needed. Maybe even teach them how to pitch an investment idea to a friend or family member. Get creative to get your child excited about a business, owning something that generates money, spending money to make money. Cost and funding. Last but possibly the singlehandedly most important decision in creating a product or service is PRICE POINT. How many cups of lemonade at what price must a kid sell to turn a profit? If success is the goal, sticking with it will determine success. So many people start and end with an idea. It's the 2 percent of people who go out there that save the money for the materials, plan out and prep the product, put a chair and a table out, and sell the lemonade. If you have ideas or you have kids with ideas, help bring them to life. Take it insanely seriously.

BEING THE BEST YOU

WE ALL HEARD it. Eat healthy, live healthy, be healthy. I don't always eat well. I was a girl who thought people took eating healthy way too seriously. I felt if you weren't obese, why do you care? I learned it wasn't always about looking healthy. Its about being and feeling healthy. I needed all the energy I could get to keep up with a kid, family, house, work, school, and my own brand investing ideas. I can't put everything I have into everything I love if I'm fatigued and tired all the time from not sleeping or eating well. I can't perform at 100 percent. I came to the table 50 percent early on because I didn't have the energy, or I didn't make time to invest in myself. How could you finish or complete anything at 50 percent? Who would want to partner or invest with someone who only has 50 percent to offer? I personally want someone who works just as hard as me and puts forth just as much as me. It's about people's expectations of the value I must add to their life. I must go the extra mile to make sure I'm eating, sleeping, and hydrating like a winner so I can be at 100 percent for those who believe in me.

LOCKUP PERSPECTIVE

PEOPLE ALWAYS ASK, "How did you feel getting locked up? What was that like?" When the courts removed me from everything, I thought I knew, into an environment that was completely new to me, they were taking a major risk. This type of experience has profound effects on children, good or bad. Other kids were not so lucky. I witness kids in their last week before they were leaving attempt to kill themselves. I always heard stories of suicide and felt if someone really wanted to do it, there was probably no way to stop them. I work for the local mental health agency and know now that is very untrue, but it's what I thought at the time. The experience of witnessing two completely different kids attempt suicide was life-changing. Their eyes were not filled with fear. It was a scary experience. It was almost like they didn't have a choice and were angry about it. It was the quick responses from staff that probably saved those kids life. Both kids ended up running away from the residential. At times, the staff would let us outside to play, or when you made it to the highest level of trust, they would take you off the unit as we called it. I watched a lot of kids come and go during my time there. I always think I'm too tough for everything. I felt it wasn't that bad on me. I didn't even like my home, but I still wanted to go home. The little corner of the world I came from made me feel "troubled," yet I knew I mentally was not in the same space as the kids around me. I had things I wanted to work toward. I had this time to work on myself. I had time to think about my future and what I want out of this world.

MY FIRST REAL ESTATE DEAL

THERE ARE PLENTY of first-time buyer horror stories or some first-time investor stories basically stating them getting some insane return on their money on their first buy. Mines were quite different. My down payment on my first property was $2,500. I know, sounds like something from the 1920s. Who can buy a house for $2,500? I did! It wasn't a very "pretty" house, but it was move-in ready. When I say move-in ready, I mean, the house had a roof, floors, walls, plumbing, electricity, and heat. It was important everything works. When looking at an investment property to buy, check the furnace; water heater; plumbing like the sinks, drains, toilet, tub; and electric. Is the electric an old tub and knob? Or is it up to date with a breaker box? These are hands down the most important things to look at physically on the house. It was priced below in my local market because it wasn't so pretty. It was a two-bedroom, one-bath, bungalow-style home. All original fixtures and door handles. All I did was replace a sink in the bathroom and a new showerhead for the tub. I had it cleaned out and rented twelve days after I closed on the purchase. Recap, I had to put 3 percent of the purchase price down. Purchase price was about $35,000. The bank paid the full amount minus my $2,500, and I owe the bank for thirty years. Well, if I can find a tenant or multiple tenants over the thirty years, they will be the one paying that debt back for the next thirty years. I put that $2,500 down and made $1,700 back twelve days after purchase. That was first month's rent and deposit from a tenant. Their rent was $850 every month after that. I knew at that moment I wanted to save for another house.

To make this deal even sweeter, this two-bedroom house had a huge attic space upstairs from the living room. My vision at purchase was to maybe, possibly, create a third bedroom in the future. It hadn't even been a whole year since I bought the property before my vision was a reality. I found some local handyman, paid them to put up some drywall, lay some laminate flooring, and build a banister at the top of the staircase. Just a couple of grand for me and that was done. There was already a heater vent leading to the attic and electricity running to a light bulb in the middle of the attic, so I knew there was already wiring done.

There are so many benefits to a deal like this. Make a third bedroom and the average person will say that's great added value to the price of the house when you get ready to sell. Sell? When? In thirty years or sooner? What if I told you I could now go to the bank and ask them for a refinance? They will revaluate the deal and the property valuation and give me the difference. They gave me three options: a cash buyout or appraise the home and they will make an offer that will pay your first mortgage and give you 80 percent of what's left. Last, they said they could give me a revolving line of credit for the same amount. I use it and pay it back as many times as I like. It's exactly what I did with my first property. I could use it whenever I needed, or I didn't have to at all. Either way, I don't pay until I pull the funds from the credit line account. Plus, I didn't disturb my first mortgage with creating the line of credit. My mortgage payments remained the same. To drop the icing on the cake, I was able to adjust rent rates from $850 to $950 with adding a third bedroom.

There were so many benefits to my first deal. It just didn't go wrong for me. I still own this property till this day.

WITH GREAT REWARD COMES
GREAT SACRIFICE

HAVE SOME PASSION for yourself. Be excited about your future because no one else cares. Understand that if I don't do anything, there is someone else out there willing to put in 150 percent every day all day. They will win. This didn't happen to me in one giant step but rather a ton of little ones. My first buy was in 2017. It's 2020, and I'm not even close to where I want to be, but I have a million people who think I'm doing just fine. They have no idea. I want it that much. I woke up one day at a time with three things to do a day that moved me toward building the empire I desire. I wake up excited every day. I smile about everything every day. I'm not saying I never have a bad day or week, or horrible things don't happen to me, but I will not let them define me. I experience brick walls on a regular. Some I can get around, others I can't, and I must be able to pull a lesson for the future out of it. That's reality. We can't break down to nothing every time something happens to us. I still get up every day excited to take the day on. It's important we're happy with what we do every day, or it's going to be hard to get up. I love to be able to pay my bills and still have the freedom to do what I want. I love interacting with people, and giving them a place to call home makes it all worth it. Bills are the reality for most of us. I found real estate to help me with that. Something I didn't have to wake up every day at 7:00 a.m. and drag myself to desk I couldn't stand for eight hours. Rent was due on the first whether I slept or was awake. I'm not as stressed about my bills anymore. I found real estate to help me with that, but I had to sacrifice. I worked a lot for little pay. I still saved that little pay and cut back on spending money on things I did not need. I had to sacrifice. Save to invest. I saved and kept a positive, friendly attitude to get to where I am now. Hanging out with our friends and spending money will always be there. Being broke is the consequence of going out and having a good time all the time. I had to sacrifice it all to build my dreams. I chose real estate.

I'm still working an 8–5 p.m. I just graduated from Western Michigan University with a bachelor's in accountancy, 2020 coronavirus graduate. I have family and friends. I'm trying to write a book, finish college, go to work, and pick up real estate along the way. I'm also engaging and consulting with folks of all ages. Mostly, they want to know how I did it, and my passion comes from telling them how they can do it too. We have so many excuses for ourselves, but we don't know we can push our bodies and minds a lot further than we think. We first must sacrifice and then save our money. Don't just save to save. Save to invest.

MY CIRCLE

MANY OF US young teens or young adults have a difficult time with who our "real" friends are and who are not. Parents will try to convince or even forcibly try to stop us from hanging with "friends" they don't approve of. Big mistake if the child is not agreeing. As parents, we are our child's best role model. If they have a good foundation of right or wrong, they should be able to make good decisions on their own. They're not perfect, and we can't protect them from everything. We can help guide them to make better choices or to think things through harder. Teach them why it's important to hang around five millionaires instead of five people who dropped out of school and have nothing of ownership. My whole life I wasn't surrounded by millionaires, didn't even know one. I guess my aunt and uncle were close enough to what I thought was a millionaire. They were and are far from it. I didn't have people around me challenging me to be the best me. They all wanted to see who was tougher. Who could fight the best? Who had the most respect, and who feared who? I may have won every question, but I was the only one who ended up in lockup with nothing. When I finally made it out, I surrounded myself with people who had goals. People who had ambition. People who created companies and legacies for themselves. They were hungry. They worked for it day in and day out. It's a contagious energy and type of conversation young people don't get to have where I came from. Just try and find people to be around who are accomplishing things in their life, building empires, and living the life that you crave. Hang out with five millionaires and watch the sixth one grow. They have the wisdom and the knowledge to pass along. Don't just be around them. Ask questions. Engage in creating value for them. Just absorb what they have to say. Model what they did to be successful.

Even on a smaller scale, it's all about influence to drive it home. Friend 1 wakes up every day and works on their résumé for twenty minutes a day and heads out to hand them out to local businesses by walking. Friend 2 has a car that their parents paid off but no job. If friend 1 can influence friend 2 to job hunt and build something too, they are ten times more likely to fill out applications, and friend 1 no longer has to walk. Now whether the argument will be is friend 2 a stronger influence and will have friend 1 no longer looking for work. I'll put my money on friend 1's influence. Friend 1 put in more work to get a résumé to a business, and I highly doubt they're willing to let that go. They had a motivation that a car wasn't even stopping them. I doubt they'll let a friend with a car stop them.

USE MY 9–5 TO BUILD MY DREAMS

MAJORITY CHOSE THIS book because they want to know how I overcame struggles and pursued real estate along the way. You want the insight. You want to know what helped me overcome childhood traumas and made me go after my dreams, to be successful.

I got tired of living paycheck to paycheck. I wanted to be worry-free of bills. I wanted to build something that created wealth. I wanted to build a brand. I wanted to invest my money into something that brought me money, an asset. I was tired of things taking money out of my pocket and not much coming in. I wanted to pick my own hours. I got tired of doing what I am told. All these reasons make me and plenty of others leave their day job, their 9–5 p.m.

You should want to leave your 9–5 day job to create your own empire. Go by your own rules. Create something to pass through your family and take care of others.

I always kick it to folks like this: why would any of us ever want to get up every day, work 9–5 p.m. every day, forty hours a week, for sixty-five years before you can enjoy time at home, time with you family, time to work on yourself and projects you've been dying to do? I want to do those things much earlier than retirement. I want to spend time with my family during the day, during the week. I want to be home for supper and reading a bedtime story. These day jobs rob us of all this time for so many years. Is that what you want for yourself and your family? Companies promise you money after taking sixty-five years of your life. No wonder people think money is evil. Thinking about it in these terms makes it sure feel evil.

I've chosen to work a 9–5 day job this entire time I've been investing in real estate. I've wanted and used the extra money to save a little quicker, to invest quicker. I used the extra money to build my brand,

LivBetter. I chose to work 9–5 p.m., five days a week, go to WMU class three to four times a week, complete homework, take care of home, cook and clean, write, create, network, plan, and set new goals and steps to accomplish them. I needed money to live and money to save along the way. Money to invest in real estate. Money to pay for a logo, business cards, a website, photography, T-shirts, and publishing a book.

Money doesn't buy happiness. You heard that before? Can you have money and be happy? I've never been happier with my family being healthy and my bills paid. Blessed enough, financially free enough to have a choice in what we do every day. Using multiple streams of income or lumps of money to take care of my family and generations to come is my dream. I had to be smart about my income from my 9–5 job. I had to cut out a lot of unnecessary spending. I had to stay home most weekends. I had to tell friends no a lot. It's tempting to go out and have fun, but fun costs money. I want my dreams more. Fun will always be around. Put yourself in a position to have fun with the least amount of work and stress.

If you work 9–5 p.m. and work on building your dream 6–11 p.m., you won't have time for the bullshit anyways. Keep spending money. If you do what you've always done, you'll get what you always gotten.

FAILURE

THAT NERVOUS LUMP in your stomach is fear. Fear of failing. You can't be scared of failure. You have to push through that feeling, and whatever happens, happens. If you fail, you try something else or come up with another way to make it happen.

I found comfort in knowing I don't have nothing to lose. If I never had nothing, how could I be scared of losing everything? I go back to where I was, zero, so what? If you grew up like me, you know that feeling. I've already had zero. I've spent my last dollar before. I can't be scared of something I already know all to well.

College was scary for me because I never felt like I was very book smart. I know people. I don't do well on tests. I failed college classes. Not one and not just two. People fear what might happen if they fail a class. They will stop coming to class, give up all together, and end up owing thousands of dollars back to the college. They would rather take the worst course of action before they finish out a failing class. They don't know they can just go back and retake it the next semester. So many students enroll each semester you won't even see any of the same classmates in that same class again unless they failed too. No shame there.

Who cares I didn't pass a class in college? I couldn't let fear of failure hold me back. I failed classes in college, and when I found out, I cried. It was hard to accept, yet that didn't stop me from facing it again. Students will change their whole major and add years to their college journey to avoid failing a class. I learned and retained way more the second time around.

Failure is a part of the journey. If I don't fail, I haven't learned. If I haven't learned, I haven't advanced my skills. How we bounce back from failure determines where we go in this life. What will we do when we face it?

PARENTS SET THEIR KIDS UP FOR FAILURE

I HAD $10 TO spend in Payless when I was a little girl in middle school on shoes. Other kids got name brand shoes that cost $100. I hated it. I always was made fun of and wasn't proud of how I grew up. Kids and society glorify how much you pay for the items you have instead of asking someone who can afford it, how they got it. You might find out if you start asking people how they bought certain expensive items they have; you will find out they actually can't afford it. Probably shouldn't have bought it.I didn't understand how at the time not having the "nice things" would motivate me in the future to build wealth for myself and my family, but it also put me at an advantage over the other kids.

Kids who had parents that paid for $100 shoes growing up don't stop at $100 shoes. Kids always want more. If parents can buy it, kids want it. Let's take shoes for instance. A parent will buy their child name brand shoes that increase in price the bigger the shoes are. So a name brand shoe that was $40–$60 is now $120 at age ten.

Have you ever heard anyone say, "I'm not paying for your shoes no more. They cost too much now"? How do you think that same kid feels after being used to getting that expensive brand? That kid grows up thinking the important things in life are keeping up with designer, and they have to find a way to come up with the money to buy it. Those same kids grow into teenagers with nothing to do in the small poor neighborhood, wondering how to make some money but without a financially educated mentor to show them the blueprint to creating wealth for themselves the right way.

They will go to the streets to try and make it any way they know how. They learn criminal ways to make money first. They will steal, scam, and sell whatever they have to. They need the money to keep up the expensive brand status.

Parents have to think about setting their kids up for success. I'm not telling parents they can't buy anything nice for their kids. I'm telling them to make sure to teach kids how to be financially free. How to invest in something that puts money back their pocket. Something the world can know about and they can be proud of.

BUILDING A TEAM

IT'S CRUCIAL TO build a reliable quality team. It's by far not easy. Again, not everyone will have your same passion or energy on a specific project. As a kid, I always thought I should only have one best friend I do everything with. That tough person mentality again. I only need one ride or die type of friend. It was only when I wanted to build this empire did I realize that it wasn't realistic thinking in the real estate world. We have to show our teens and young adults how false this really is. I was twenty-five years old with real estate. I needed someone who knew how to hang drywall, I needed one who knew about plumbing and water heaters, I needed one who knew electric and wiring, and I needed someone who knows how to lay floor and trim. I have to be open to ideas and new people. Just saying hi to everyone I pass or see won't produce productivity for me, but it's a good business practice. It is having some manners, common courtesy. I never know who I may be speaking to and what kind of opportunity awaits. Get comfortable talking to people, even if it's saying hi to every single person I pass today. Not all of them will speak back, and that's okay too. That's not a reflection of you. When something needs to be repaired or fixed at a property, I don't just talk to one person about everything. I have to engage with multiple people. I run things by multiple workers. Real estate is much like having a car. Something goes wrong with the car, auto body shops have to troubleshoot and figure out the issue. Same in real estate, I run issues by more than one person all the time. One of them might have a real good idea as to what could be going wrong and what we can do to fix it. I trust their opinion. I have to. They are the experts in what they do. Me and my one best friend can't run this whole company, or I'll run myself into the ground. Building a team has many different players. I had to think about which bank to use. Who will the realtor be to show me the houses? Who are my potential workers on the project? I don't want anyone who's reading this book think that I would ever tell them to do everything themselves. Work smart, not harder. It takes way too much time to do everything ourselves. If you have a million dollars worth of real estate, will you go out and collect rent every month door to door? That's not realistic. Maybe not knowing where to find these people is the issue. Open your mouth. Start talking. Walk and breathe real estate. They will find you too. Connect with people online who have the same passion. We have access to everyone in the world. People will be at all different stages of real estate. Some may have one property, maybe two. Some will have thirty or more. Maybe someone with an apartment complex or commercial property. All of them will talk about mistakes, success, past or present issues, and everything in between. They will help you unintentionally along the way.

BUILDING A BRAND

I HAD TO learn that my brand is my reputation. I was building my brand the wrong way all my childhood. For six years in my young teen life, I chose to get into trouble. I chose to catch those criminal charges. I was out there fighting and disrespecting anyone around me. My decisions were building my brand without my knowledge. Who wants to invest with someone who might be involved in criminal activity? People will sit and watch you for years before they invest, or they might not ever. Their word to other people means a lot whether they're true. We have to put as much good in this world as we want out. We have to make people know we are good people too. We want everyone to win as cheesy as it may sound. If we all win, we all can't lose, but I determine with my actions how people will view me and my brand. To grow a brand or business, I had to buy into my own dreams. I needed other people to buy into my dreams. I had to ask myself, what does my brand represent? What does my name say? No one's to risk their investing deals with a person who could singlehandedly take them down with all their bad decisions and disrespect. I had to find something to live kindly for. Something that changed the way I responded to people and situations. Slowly, I began to build a platform and a network of people who have seen all the hard work and years I put into rebranding myself to prove I'm someone who can change despite what I've been through. I started with a job. Maybe you want to start with a small startup like selling T-shirts or washing cars. There is a blueprint to this whole idea of branding. Find a good mentor or coach. Create a website maybe, create a logo, start with selling and marketing to your friends and family, create flyers, write books, brand clothing, attach meaning to your brand. I had to push my brand on various platforms—social media, websites, storefronts, and seminars. I had to do market research on each platform. Who am I targeting, and How do I find them? This brand building, again, is not one giant step. I started with one job and saving, and then college and saving, and then one property and saving, and then writing a book to sell, and then creating T-shirts with my logo to sell, and then creating a website, and then creating a social media to market from. Use this framework to brand and build the business you want. Help show someone else.**What Is Your Self-Talk?**

Self-talk, or thoughts in your head, will make or break future hopes and dreams—literally. I challenge everyone around me to find some positive spin on some shitty day. Every bad or negative thought ruins a future. Being around negative thoughts and energy can suck the life out of you. Stay clear of those people. I can talk until I'm blue in the face, and it won't make it difference. They want to be mad, let them be mad, but don't let it be you.

I hear people come into work every day complaining about being there, having to get up, how much work there is to do. Well, if I didn't have an exit plan, I would have a hard time accepting I'm going to be sitting in the same chair for thirty years too. They come to this job with no intentions of ever leaving. It's a death sentence. Someone else holds their paycheck every week, and they have them by the throat. Who wouldn't have negative self-talk? That's why successful people talk about finding your passion. It's about finally having the freedom to hire someone else to do the work, having the freedom to not work at all that day. Maybe I wanted to work four hours a week and still receive my pay. Don't let the position you're in today define your future.

Imagine someone smiling every day, thankful they woke up, going above and beyond to help people around them. We all can't stand that 8–5 p.m., we have the same exact job, I just chose to plan an exit to keep me happier in between. Find the purpose. Use your 9–5 to finance that purpose in life. My days are much shorter and lighter. I still have energy to go home and work on my own dreams. They barely have energy to go home and play with their own kids. That negative self-talk drains people. I know. I had a lot of them. I ended up too tired to cook, clean, and do laundry most days. My self-talk was limiting me from reaching my full potential.

HEALTHY VERSUS UNHEALTHY RELATIONSHIPS

WHO DO YOU surround yourself with? Who does our children surround themselves with? Who are we talking to every day? Mom? Dad? Kids? Friends? Who are they? What do they talk about? Cars? Money? Real estate? Investing? Business? Partying? Stealing? What about our kids? Do you even know who they surround themselves with? Whoever we decide to surround ourselves with and what we talk about determines our lifestyle. I'm not saying one or two conversations here and there with loved ones will bring you down or create an impact we can't come back from. I'm talking about that person or people you talk to the most. Every day. What do they do for a living? What do you all talk about?

If I go around someone who always have something negative to say, how they can't do this, no one likes them, and they can't do that. They never have enough money to get by. Someone who still wants to go out though on the weekend and maybe even fight someone. So that's about what I can expect to come from that relationship. I'm not talking about the 1 percent who can be themselves no matter who they hang with. A total of 99 percent of us are who we associate ourselves with. If you hang around five people with a car, job, and crib, you will be the sixth person with a car, job, and crib. If you want healthy relationships, hang out with people who want more than you out of life. Let them inspire you. Watch how they conduct themselves. Don't be the parent who calls their kid out for the one friend they have you think don't live up to your expectations. Show them the future relies heavily on who they hang out with and what those people will or won't accomplish.

START A LITTLE, FINISH A LOT

PEOPLE ASK ME all the time the secret to "troubled youth." How do we get young people activated? What's the secret to success? I can't emphasis enough to just take one step at a time. I started a little at a time and finished a lot. Everyone's goals should have at least five steps or more to obtain them. I never took on an unrealistic amount of responsibility that was too overwhelming. I was doing enough as it was. I could never overcomplicate a situation. Even this book, every day I would try and write a little bit down. I ended up writing pages after pages. One thought to tell you guys something led me to another thought. I was surprised how much I kept writing. I naturally started to push myself to keep going. It just had to be a want big enough for me to achieve. The result was my motivation.

If we even take the goal to washing dishes or doing laundry, I would start with pulling out and rinsing off dishes, unfolding, and sorting out laundry. Start the washer with laundry soap. Fill the sink up with hot water and dish soap. Every single thing we do has five steps big or small.

It works exactly the same in real estate or branding a business. Want to sell a T-shirt? What kind of shirt will I buy? What screen printing company am I going to use? What will be on the shirt? Who will design what I want on the shirt? How much will it cost? How many to sell, and what price to turn a profit? How will I market them? Who will I sell to?

Small steps, starting a little will help ease the overwhelming stress of how much there is to do. Tackling one thing, one question at a time set me up to finish a lot.

POOR MONEY MANAGEMENT

JUST BECAUSE I make a lot of money doesn't mean I how to manage it and make more. It doesn't mean I know how to make money smart purchases with my profit. I should only spend my money if that money goes out and gets me more money.

Pick any sports league. I'll say football. These players get paid millions of dollars to play for a few years. There was some crazy statistic that came out saying majority of these players end up broke or bankrupt five years after their contract ended. How many of you would blow through millions of dollars in five years? You mean to tell me you didn't spend $1 that gave you a return? For me, this is insane! This is self-suicide. This may shock some people, and you may have to go look it up. I do know now these leagues are acting. They make every player take some type of money management/finance course before signing contracts. This shit is real. Money management is that important. I can't spend the money as fast as it comes in. I can't live up to my every last dollar and think it's never going to rain.

Unfortunately for some of the earlier players, they didn't see a future in investing or any kind of exit plans. They only think one thing, football. What they don't count on is an injury ever happening. Understanding the likelihood of an injury happening. It happens a lot in sports. They don't see past playing forever. They get old, and someone younger, stronger, faster comes along. Worst part about it all, they spent all their money by the time it happened, or they figured it all out. They invested wrong. They went out and bought the biggest house with the most bills and highest taxes, bought not one but multiple high-end expensive cars and the rest on their luxury lifestyles and expensive clothes.

I had to look at money differently. I had to view anything going out that's not coming back is an expense, a liability. An asset was anything going out and bringing me back more! Their house was not an asset. My rental properties are assets. Not our dream home like they tell us in school. They don't teach us real life money management skills in school. We have to go out and find the education ourselves.

HOME-IMPROVEMENT STORE EXPERIENCES

ANYONE WHO HAS been to the local hardware or home-improvement store? Whew! That has been quite the adventure! I don't think five years later it's gotten any easier.

I went to the store to get light switch covers three times. For beginners in real estate, you probably haven't even thought of light switch covers. If you did, you're already ahead of where I started. I've experience getting the wrong materials more times than the right ones. I still didn't let a home-improvement store scare me. A twenty-five-year-old young lady in a hardware store. Searching for materials for rental property improvements. Most times, I feel undercover. No one would ever guess why I'm in this store. I couldn't be scared of the store. Guess what, men go in there and grab the wrong things all the time. It's not a woman or man thing at this point. It's a home-improvement store and a home repair project trying to get done.

As long as I had the Internet and the website YouTube.com, I couldn't lose. There is a video online right now about how to do anything. You complete the sentence. How to sing, how to tie a shoe, how to spend a coupon, how to put up drywall, how to refurnish wood floors, how to get started in real estate home-improvement projects. The videos are endless! The Internet also helps network for people who have been doing these kinds of things for thirty-plus years. Finding someone I could pay to do it was an option for me. I was money smart. I collect rent and make sure it gets to the bank account. I don't do repairs that are needed. I don't do repairs on my own home I live in unless it's needed. Don't get too attached to these investments. They are there to make you money.

Not only the Internet, but also the people right in my face at the store had a ton a knowledge around the best products to use and their knowledge around the project. Everything you do to maintain a property has to be learned through experience or others. I could get experts around me to tell me about things I didn't know or do work I've never done.

Everyone has a skill to offer. I need to be able to organize the deal and execute the plans. I need someone else to come in and replace a furnace. I need someone else to come in and wire a house. Could I spend the time to learn how to replace a furnace? Could I spend the time learning how to rewire a whole house? If I did that, who's going to organize the deal and execute the plans? It's impossible for us to do everything ourselves. I have to rely on others in my real estate investments. If I want to be a millionaire one day, I can't keep thinking so small. We need a village to raise a child. What do we need to build an empire?

MAKING TIME WHEN THERE AIN'T NO TIME

LIFE WRAPS US up and swallows us whole sometimes. I was a mother with a son. I know many can relate to how much time we have to ourselves. I had to go to work to pay bills and survive. I had to make time to educate myself, my son; hang and enjoy time with my family; cook for a family; clean; and do laundry. This is 99 percent of parents out here. We have to decide for ourselves to be the 1 percent. I want to be the 1 percent. The 1 percent that makes time for her own dreams, makes time to build a brand. I'm guilty of playing harder than investing. I've had to carry so much for so long I'd make excuses. I found time for other things. I had to make the decision that I wanted something that would last more than a minute or two. I want something that would last for generations. That would carry long after I'm gone. I chose to cut back on those purchases and putting more time into creating value for my family.

We hear from adults all the time that it doesn't matter how much, just save anything, $10. Let me be the first to say if you haven't already heard. You ain't going nowhere on that $10. I had to sacrifice hundreds of dollars a month, $500 a month until I reached $10,000 and didn't use but a quarter of it. I had plenty left over for a rainy day on my investment.

I had to make the time to research the local real estate market, make plans to obtain a property. Follow through on those plans. I was disciplined enough to make time for my dreams in 2016 and had a property by 2017 when I made time for my dreams.

BUILDING WEALTH WITHIN THE
HOUSEHOLD IN REAL ESTATE

I HAVE TO share one way my family went outside the box to figure out how we could get to the next level. One of us had thirty single family properties. He was pretty much ready to take it to the next level with an apartment complex. In our local real estate market, we were looking at anywhere from $200,000 to $500,000 on a down payment. As great as thirty properties cash flow is, that money isn't easy to come by starting at zero. I had just a couple of rental properties under my belt, but I did have another preapproval from the bank. A preapproval is what any realtor needs to start showing properties to me. The bank is saying on that preapproval, they have examined my finances and determined I'm eligible to help finance a property for me.How could we take our situation to the next level? We decided if he sold me one of his properties for top value, he could gain good ground toward a down payment on an apartment complex, I could get the next investment I wanted, and we could keep the cash flow all within the same household. How could we lose? We can't no matter how we looked at it. If you can find a doubt, get out now. No way you can build wealth in the same household if you guys aren't trying to get each other there together.

BALANCE

WHATEVER I DO in life always calls for the right balance. If you show too much tough love, you will push them away. As a mentor, coach, parent, friend, whatever the relationship may be. Worse, we may even push them away from their goals. The right amount will fuel them to pursue their dreams. We could make them give up or go harder in our approach. If I don't push someone enough, they won't push themselves. Worse, they may not accomplish anything.

Just like selling a product or service, if I'm too pushy, people won't buy. Everyone and everything I come into contact with must be given the right balance of me. I give them too much of me; they can't handle it. I don't give them enough; they push me away.

You have to understand people. Not one kind, all kinds. Understand the product or service you have and give the target audience a right balance to entice them to buy. Understand when you're not the person for the job too. Know your weaknesses. If people are your weakness, maybe your shouldn't be the salesman on the front line. Maybe you should be more involved when it comes to the design or development of a product.

Find the balance that serves the investment the best way possible. Hire other people to do things that aren't your strengths. That's okay. That's the point.

WHY DID I CHOOSE REAL ESTATE AND BRANDING?

PEOPLE ASK ME all the time why I chose real estate. I don't like to work for my money. What do I mean? I mean, getting up every day to put in physical work to get money out of the deal. I don't care what it is. I don't want to have to get up every day and go to a place of business to get my money. I want to put my money into something I can go to sleep at night knowing the first of the month's rent due is coming.

The stock market is too uncontrollable. I can't control my money in the market. I also barely understand the lingo when dealing with trading. If someone wants to learn that and skim off the bottom or hold money somewhere again for a crazy amount of years to get a few thousand by all means, go ahead.

When I say somewhere again, I mean, people who put and hold their money in a bank—CDS, trusts, or savings account. That investment doesn't bring you close to the return a rental property or real estate could bring you.

I chose branding because brand power is everything. If as a company you have brand power, you're at the top of the food chain. Consumers will buy whatever product their favorite brand will come out with off the strength of their brand.

I didn't realize growing up how important it is consumers view my brand or myself as someone they can count on and spend their money with. I didn't understand the power my reputation can have. People support my way more now because of the hard work I've put into rebranding my self. I started with getting out of the environment I was growing up in. I went back to school and got educated. I had a son and worked more hours a week than I got to spend with him. All so I could give him the world. People stand behind me for that. No one stood behind me when I was fighting, skipping school, selling weed, and catching charges.

I chose branding and real estate because those are the things I'm passionate about and helped me turn my life around. This gave me so much excitement for the future. I'm excited to know my son and family could be left with something to take care of the themselves with. So many times, people leave this earth, and family and friends are left with more debts and costs than financial freedom.

WHERE TO START

ITS NOT THAT I wasn't motivated. I've been motivated all my life. I just didn't have the blueprint. I didn't know what this all meant. I didn't know where to start.

First, what am I doing? Selling a product? Providing a service? I chose real estate and a motivational empire. Real estate has a different route from building a motivational empire.

I started with a logo that people could attach to my brand. I created a social media site to promote my brand and lifestyle on. I created content like clothing and books to reach a broader audience. I want to start a podcast or video content platform to get people activated to think about their future. I created business cards to pass to other professionals. I consult with anyone willing to discuss their dreams and how to obtain them. I could create more. I could create a Q and A platform to reach more people and answer more questions directly related to their lives.

The moral of the story is figuring out where to start to focus in at, and the rest will be a snowball effect. I didn't know I needed something until I needed it, and it was too late. Missed opportunity, but you learn these things and adjust along the way. I started with working that forty-hour-week job and going to college just like everyone else. I used it to start to build what I have now. I made time to build and promote myself. It sounds like common sense, but we're told while in school to just focus on school, just focus on completing high school, just focus on what college you want to go to. We should've been told about investing, building wealth, creating content and brands.

Tell us it will be a lonely road to start. We cut out fun and friends to get somewhere, but we pick up new ones along the way. I am 100 percent against doing it all alone for twenty years. You must know your exit plan before getting into it. How will I be able to step back from an investment and still make money?

WHAT I DID WITH MY COLLEGE MONEY

I DON'T THINK SOMEONE needs college at all to be successful. Someone can have learned some valuable skills during years in college but nowhere near enough skills to be $100,000 in debt. To go to a job that takes your money through taxes before you even see it. Investors collect their money first and pay the government their money later. I do not think college is for everyone, but society has made it normal for the masses. We tell a lot of people to go to college. How many people do you know went to college? Did you go to college? Did you or anyone you know end up leaving college with a lot of debt? Unless you were one of those 1 percent who went on Pell grants and scholarships. Most of us took federal loans. When I first started college, my college money went on daily living expenses like rent, food, car repairs, and our son. The rest I blew through on going out, drinking, partying, buying clothes and food. I was a mom who had a $500 rent a month working two part-time jobs that was paying minimum wage of around $8 an hour, going to college part time, and walking to and from work. I had no help from the state and still had a good amount of money after taking care of all our basic needs. I wasted a lot of loan money to start. I'm sure many could relate, or maybe it's just me? After a few semesters of wasting money, I decided to take my money and save it to go on that first property I wanted.

I also put my college money with money I got back in taxes at the end of the year for that down payment on my first property. Now I know many average people can relate to running across tax money. Too many times we waste it. Yes, we also pay up on bills and catch up old ones, but instead of thinking about investing big lumps of money, we spend it on stupid shit that doesn't bring us a dollar in return.

There are thousands of people who go to my college that get them school loans. Many get taxes. We all end up broke a month later. I had to get tired of that. I had to see it was a vicious cycle to be in. Be smart. Find some people and spread the word. Pitch investment deals to your friends and family. Invest in the materials or property you need to get started. We come across money even coming from nothing. We just don't see the opportunity it has. We don't see the potential of investing the money.

FINANCIAL DISCIPLINE

I TOUCHED EARLIER on the fact we've all heard someone in our life tell us to save "anything we can." How many times have you heard that? Do the math. Let's say you save $5 a week. It would take you four years to save $5,000. Two years saving $10 a week. That may not sound that long to you. What's the chances you will need some of that money in the next two years when you're living paycheck to paycheck? I had to save close to 50 percent of all the income I had coming in. We all spend money on stuff we don't need. It's human. I had to cut out all that unnecessary spending.

Some people really spend for no reason at all. I worked with a girl who had two kids. She was paying $300 a week in day care expenses. Most people can relate. Most struggle to get a job for this reason alone. Day care is expensive. She was also saving $20 a week. She just couldn't figure out how to get ahead.

Our job has a childcare reimbursement program. All she has to do is turn in her receipts. It was the only thing holding her back from saving $300 a week. Sounds crazy, but it happens all the time. Stressed, too thin to try and figure anything out.

That $20 fund she was using every time she got behind in life. It wasn't her fault; it's life. I can help people point these things out in their life, but they have to be the one to follow through.

THE BANK AND INSURANCE AGENCIES

I F YOU GET started in real estate when you have limited funding, no doubt, you will deal with the bank and the people who will insure your property. It is intimidating. They are people who give you the funding to go after your dreams. I felt I had to go with whatever they say so they help me. What I didn't think was, if they don't say yes, there's a million other banks to try. If my paperwork is good, my credit score is good, my financials are in order, there isn't much a bank wouldn't do to work with me. They want business. Don't be afraid to ask questions throughout the process. Ask for your options as a borrower. Everything is negotiable.

Don't be afraid to call them. If they get ahold of you every time, they need additional information. Don't be scared to call them back in a few days to see how things are coming along and if there is anything else you can get them. Be kind. Be respectful. Don't be scared. Even if it doesn't work out with that bank, there is more. Just don't sit around the phone pathetic, waiting on them to call. I had to show them I was serious. I wanted them to be serious. Houses come and go fast in a good market. My market was a good market. The next persona and their lender aren't going to sit around and wait. Somebody else is on the phone with their bank or realtor, asking questions. Don't overdo it. Time it right. Give them information and give them ample time to reply yet know when it's time to call and ask some questions.

Treat these people like your family. You will make it a lot farther the kinder you treat people. The more helpful you are to a situation.

FIGHT FOR IT

DO YOU HAVE dreams? Fight for them. No one will fight for what you want in life like you will. Not your friends, family, kids, or anyone else. People will only fight for you as much as it may benefit them. I had to make sure there were people around me who had my best interest in mind, push me to be the best me. I've had people go above and beyond to make sure I'm okay.

You may not have anyone like that, but they still could never fight and live my dreams for me. I talk about everything in this book. I chose real estate. Some people know drawing, writing, designing, and engineering. Some know selling and engaging a customer. These are skills that can be turned into a dream to fight for. Any of them can be turned into a brand or company.

Maybe someone buys a location and sells their own art or other people's art. Maybe they sell books. Maybe someone buys a property to sell retail items out of. People can't fight for what they don't know.

How many people do you have around you ask you about your goals in life? How many of them ask you how you are going to get there? How many of them help you get there? I know we all had those people who will ask you what you're doing this weekend. They will help you hang out and spend money but can't help you catch a ride to work. They don't have anything. They don't want to go to work. These people end up determining your fight. They don't help you save up for an investment. They don't go half on the investment with you. They don't go half on your dreams with you.

I chose to fight all my life. That was the wrong fight. This book is for them tough kids. Them kids who don't want to listen to nobody, but those kids are smart. Those kids are so smart they have it already, and they know it. We must help ourselves and young people figure out how to channel it into an investment, a brand, a business of some kind.

I suggest talking about money. They know what it can and can't do. If they're young people like me, you can't talk about good grades and behavior, they don't want to hear it. Show them money. How they can make it. Show them how to manage it. Easy to stay out of trouble if they're too busy making money. Fighting, using drugs, and stealing are bad for business. It's opposite from the street. No one wants to make money with someone they fear and can't trust.

I've been fortunate to have people later in my young adult life who have pushed me to fight for myself. They continue to pat me on my back when I'm not done fighting. Those are people I want around me as I keep fighting for success. Fight for yours whether you have those people now or you gain them on the way.

TENANT STORIES

G OT TO HAVE a good ol' tenant story!
For my first property, I chose a nice young qualified couple
with two kids to rent the property to. Both tenants worked and brought
in decent money yet seemed to be struggling to keep up with rent. Just
a few months after signing the lease, they were fighting like cats and
dogs. One tenant called me one day and was requesting I come over
and call the cops on the other tenant on the lease. Huh? That's just to
warm ya'll up.

It wasn't hard to get them to move. They just picked up one day
and left without paying rent before there was even a court date issued.
They did give me my keys back but left the house a mess. They left me
plenty of work to keep me busy for the next two weeks.

I had another tenant move into that same property. They called
me one day frantic. "Liv! You need to get over here right now and do
something!" I asked what was going on. Their reply was "There are
flies all over my house, and I have no idea where they came from, but
they are everywhere!"

I couldn't make this up. I didn't take these kinds of calls into account
when I decided I was going to pursue real estate. I got a lot of calls like this
from that tenant during their stay. After a while, I did get a little burned
out with them, and it was hard to figure out a real landlord responsibility
from a fake one. Maybe it should be just a reminder to what tenant
responsibility is and be sure it's in the lease. I still had to check out every
complaint they made. I wanted to make sure I was fulfilling my duties as
a landlord and make sure my house was taken care of.

Again, like the first story, one day the tenant told me they would
pay me the following week for rent that was due the current week, but
it didn't happen. Instead, I received a letter from an attorney's office.
It was claims from the tenant, claims that I did not complete repairs.

Honestly, I was confused. I bent over backward to make sure complaints were taken care of. I did not see that coming. They never told me about any of the complaints that were documented in the letter. The letter also stated they were not planning on paying rent, and they were planning on fighting me in court.

Court came, and they had already moved out once again and just wanted to give me the keys back. Again, weird. By the time I got possession of my property back, I was a little nervous to what I might find. How did the tenant leave my house?

Long story short, the tenant had brought a large fish tank into the house and on to the second floor. I'm not exactly sure how it happened, but a large amount of water spilled across the upstairs floor. So much water that much of it pooled up against the board joints in the floor. It was so heavy it bubbled downstairs in the living room ceiling, eventually breaking through the ceiling in the living room. It wasn't as bad as it sounds; it really wasn't that bad. It could have been worse.

My assumption is the tenant did not want to find out how bad that was going to be on them. They'd rather pack their stuff up and move.

How about a lesson from someone who wasn't a tenant? I was showing an available three-bedroom house I had for rent. I had a decent amount of people want to see it and fill out an application.

One couple gave me security deposit to just hold it until the end of the week. They seemed pretty serious to me. They said they would have first month's rent by that Friday. At the end of the week, one of them called me and wanted to know if they could get their deposit back because they had got approved somewhere else. They really wanted it and finally heard back.

My lesson, I never told them their security deposit was nonrefundable. I was a new investor and made a mistake. I've learned more doing than I did reading any books. Books helped me get motivated and understand process better. Nothing is like hands-on experience. I did give them back their deposit, but it won't happen like that again. I was holding people off all week. I told them someone had put security deposit down. We all thought it was gone. I had to then start over and reshow the property and go over applications.

I couldn't make this up. Those same people called me a couple of weeks later requesting to rent the same house. That house had already been rented out by then. I wouldn't have rented to them if it was available. I would be too worried they would do that when the rent is due. Will they even pay? Will they leave and go pay someone else one month? I couldn't take another risk like that. I'm still trying to make it and have a family to feed.

It's a tight, dangerous rope at times to walk with tenants. There is an overwhelming belief a landlord can eat losses and be okay. The houses I invest in aren't free. There are expenses associated with ownership of a property. Most landlords make little to no money on their investments because they have too many expenses and aren't collected enough in rent to make it. They are spread too thin. They have $500 a month in expenses and rent their property out for $650–$700 in my local area. That's not enough. To replace an interior door cost over $100. I hope for their sake, a furnace doesn't go out, their setback over a year. Or a water heater. That $100–$200 a month won't cover all the maintenance and unforeseen occurrences that happen. It comes with ownership. Being business and profit minding when created price versus cost.

One call from the tenant for something will eat that margin and some. Our margins determine if we can survive during the low times. What we do with our rent collections will determine if we can survive and grow.

One expense people like to think as the dark side, evil is insurance. People hate insurance companies. I'm here to tell you in real estate that's your friend.

I had more than one tree in one month fall on my properties during bad windstorms one year. I had a couple living in one. I woke up one morning to five missed calls from this tenant. Come to find out an enormous tree that the city owned had fallen on top of the house and completely crushed their car in the driveway.

Something I've never saw before. I was completely shocked; it was definitely a freak accident. Thank God, no one was hurt. A house and a car could be replaced, a life, not so much. I had insurance on my house. I just had to call my insurance company. They sent someone out

     LIVIA WORLEY

to estimate the damages and then, a few days later, cut me a check to get my roof fixed. It just damaged a couple of rafters, and the rest was in good condition.

The tenant had a car in the driveway they had been using but no insurance on it. It was a complete lost, and they completely lost out. Yes, they could've sued the city, but that takes money too. Attorney costs are not cheap, and if they can't afford insurance payments monthly, I don't think they can afford to defend themselves in court.

I wanted to help. I tried to see if there was anything I could do under my policy for them, but there wasn't. Their lesson is insurance. Even if they had the lowest coverage, they would've been paid out completely for the value of the car. It's considered property damage if no one was driving it at the time. The lowest coverage has that policy coverage in Michigan. There was nothing I could do for them.

Understandably, after that, they stopped paying rent. They left the house in complete filth though. It seems they just came and went as they pleased for two months. Didn't pick up or clean anything. Bringing tons of fast food and cooking, but not one thing had been cleaned. No soap and water used in months. There was an awful sour garbage smell as soon as I opened the front door to the property.

Believe it or not, I can't make this shit up, they took my fridge. Ha ha. It was the worst part of the whole deal for me. No rent for a couple of months, left the property filthy, and took my damn fridge. That may sound like more than most can handle, but I cleaned the house, paid $200 for a new fridge, and only lost out on one month's rent because I had their deposit to use to get the property ready for the next tenant.

The next person I put in that home paid six months in advance the day we signed the lease. It's not always bad.

These tenant stories shouldn't scare you from investing in single family or apartment complexes. I love being a real estate investor. I've experienced if I treat people well, they won't totally disappointment me. It has its moments, but I love it. I love people finding a place they can call home, and I love I can make that happen. Most people have done right by me as a landlord as long as I treat them well and uphold my duties as a landlord.

IN BETWEEN TENANTS—CREATING LEASES

I WENT OUT and got a thirty-year mortgage. Not one person will live in that house for thirty years straight. I couldn't get hung up in all the drama from tenants. They pay rent, they stay. They don't pay rent, there is a process to evict. This is simple; I won't overcomplicate it. Be an honest, good, and fair landlord. If they still don't pay rent, there is a process to evict. Stay out of going back and forth with them about anything. If they're late, serve them with the eviction papers from your local civil court office. Follow their policies strictly. They will be out before sixty days top in my local area. Get your property back and start getting it ready for the next tenant.

It's the same process no matter what. After the eviction, I would get possession of my property back. I would have to go in and take a look around, figure out what repairs were needed to bring the property back where it needs to be for the next family.

I had a tenant who was paying $850 for a two bed, one bath. She moved out and broke the lease. She did not receive her deposit back. It took me about $1,000 in repairs to get the property ready for the next family. It took me sixteen days for my first tenant turnover and received $2,500 from the next family. Cash in hand with a new qualified tenant. People wonder how to find good tenants. How do I find good contractors? How do I know I'm getting into the right deal?

Do your due diligence. Check where people work. How long have they been there? How much do they get paid? Where do they live now, and how much do they pay? How long have they lived there?

Be a good person and look things over carefully. I learned as I went with each tenant. Each tenant taught me a new thing that needed to be in the lease. I could revise it anytime between renewals or turnovers. Most of us rented before. We know what we like in our landlord and what we don't. We carry what we know and what's already out there. The Internet can give us a template or how to whenever we want. I look up templates for leases, rental applications, invoices, or any other documents I need.

HOW I USE EVICTIONS

ALL EVICTIONS I have ever filed have been for nonpayment of rent. Once I realized a tenant was not going to pay rent one month, I just file an eviction notice to start the legal process to regain possession of my property.

I understand things happen and costs out of tenants' control come up in life. I always offer tenants an option to move out voluntarily on their own and return all the sets of keys to the house, and I won't pursue an eviction. An eviction can set people back for as long as it takes for them to take care of it. It remains on their history anytime an apartment complex or management team runs their name.

Some have taken me up on the offer, and some have not. The tenants who had me go all the way through the eviction process to get my property back still have a money judgment against them, but I have not pursued collections. Landlords can put in paperwork for garnishment of wages as long as they know where the tenant currently works. It would continue until the amount owed is paid back.

My intentions were never to get my money back from those tenants. I want them to move forward with their lives, and I move on with mine.

I did have a tenant I previously evicted reach out to me months after being evicted. They had tried to recently rent from an apartment complex in the local area who could see they had an eviction on their rental history. They couldn't rent from the apartment complex until they took care of the eviction on their name. They reached out to pay the amount they owed, and they did just that.

I never intended to get my money from them or even see them ever again. I don't use evictions as a weapon against my tenants. I use it as a process to get possession of my property back.

DO SETBACKS MAKE FOR MAJOR COMEBACKS?

I USED TO let the smallest things stop me from moving forward or set me back for years. I watched people now around me who know where I came from, watched me build something for myself but can't seem to feel inspired enough to do it too.

I know people with bank accounts who took the first step letting the bank run their credit to see how close they are to being able to get approved for financing through the bank. The bank told them what was on it. It wasn't all clear, but it wasn't nothing that couldn't be fixed. They let days, even months, go by, and they lose the paper the bank gave them. They never called anyone to try and get any of the accounts fixed on it. I understand life is hard, but you can't let these things set you back for life.

I used to try and purposely think about all the people who grew up worse than me. I used to think about the people who are starving in the world, fighting for a place to just be safe. Those moments got me through my lowest moments in life. There is always someone out there who has it worse than you. Everyone starts this life at different levels, but we have to fight through all that.

Why couldn't someone get the information from the bank and follow through? Maybe you lost the paperwork? Call them back. Set up another meeting. Be honest. Tell them you lost the paperwork and you need another copy. Tell them to explain your credit and how it works. Ask them, how do you build it?

They won't tell you how to use it. They will tell you an amount you are approved for and send you on your way. It's your job to figure out your numbers to make sure you don't end up in a situation where the setback ends up taking years to correct or it's so discouraging you end up giving up.

DREAM HOUSE VERSUS FIRST HOUSE

L IVE IN SOMETHING that you can live in for a while and rent out later to start. Too many people get stuck on buying their dream home by thirty or even younger. I know so many people who are middle aged and went out and bought a house in my local market from $150,000 to $250,000. Now they have a $1,000 mortgage payment and barely making enough to scrape by. They went out and spent up to the amount the bank approved them for instead of thinking about how they could take advantage of this opportunity to bring in more money.

If it were me, I'd sell that house in a heartbeat. I'd downsize. I'd go get something affordable. That goes for new cars too. Go take it back. Get something you're not paying on every month. If you care what people think, you won't build wealth. Everyone around you will encourage you to go have fun. Enjoy yourself. I agree but only when you're financially ready.

It's already going to be hard enough to find someone to rent out a home for $1,000 or higher type of renter's market for the dream house they just spent all their money on. It's not a good opportunity to make money by the time you realize it, at least in my area.

Wait to buy that dream home. I still haven't bought my dream home. When I can afford one, I will. A total of 90 percent of Americans live in their dream house before they should.

RENTAL PROPERTIES VERSUS FLIP PROPERTIES

THERE'S ALWAYS TALK about whether to invest in rental properties or rehab and flip properties. Both can be done. That's proven. People make money in both.

I chose rental properties to start. I didn't have much capital to work with. I also think in the long run that house flipper has to go out and find that new property to flip once their done with the one they have. I could stop tomorrow, and the rent is still due on the first.

I imagine if you came from where I did, you don't have those types of funds yet. Start with a rental property. Save up anywhere from 3 percent to 20 percent of the purchase price. It was easy for me to reach. I had to make sure I knew I had to look for a move-in ready property to purchase as a rental property with no repairs needed or very few. I could then focus on listing my property and interviewing potential tenants instead spending more money.

Flip properties take a lot of work. Imagine buying a property with no walls, no furnace, no cabinets, and barely any floors. Remember, you have no money, even if you had free labor and did everything yourself. You need material costs. The flip game takes capital. I want to do that too. I just had to start somewhere else. Rentals.

When I talk to people about rental properties, there's a running theme. They don't know what they'd do if they got a call from the tenant for a needed repair. Start with looking for a move-in ready property. There are little to no repairs. Check things out as if you were going to move in. Check the water, heat, electricity. Check the sinks, tubs, and drains. Check the roof. Make sure all the walls and floors are intact. Are there appliances there? All these features will cost if they're not checked out. When you put someone in the property, they give you first month's rent and deposit. It's important you never go out and spend the rent money you get. Save it for a rainy day. You will have the money when a repair comes.

Save every rent dollar you get so you can reinvest it into another property.

Housing markets are tough to get into at times when the economy is booming. Maybe you take a house on that needed small repairs. Small repairs would be like door locks, window locks, maybe a door replacement—small repairs that can still be manageable for first-time investors.

Never buy a house you need to replace a water heater or furnace. I also tell people I personally know they can call me anytime to help figure things out. It's important to find a mentor or coach within the same industry you're joining. Rental properties that are move-in ready will always be my choice over flips for first-time investor with limited capital like myself.

LIVIA WORLEY

BEING PERSONABLE

W HEN I WAS younger, I didn't care who I connected with and who I didn't. I didn't see the value I had to offer them, and I didn't see what they could possibly offer me. I've been making decisions for myself all my life. It wasn't that I wasn't likable or relatable. I just didn't know my purpose.

Connecting with people might not be your thing anyway. You can still build a brand or invest in real estate. It will just be a longer and harder journey for you. You may even fail more times than not.

I love people. I love sparking meaningful conversations around people's goals and ambitions. Others will give you the creditability to others around you. If you go around caring about yourself and never giving back, people won't root for you. They don't care to support you. People are what makes people and investments successful.

I've worked with plenty of people who walk around mad at the world, and guess what. They've been stuck in the same position for years. Barely have people who want to interact with them. Much less go out their way to help them. No one wants to help someone who won't help themselves.

People who are kinder to others, smile more, and speak to everyone they see have more positive things happen to them in life. People will go out of their way to help good people just trying to make something for themselves.

I talk to our son about the importance of being nice all the time. No one will want to be around someone who's not nice. No one wants to be around someone who is angry all the time, complains all the time, never grateful for anything. If you invest in real estate, there's people you will need to interact with positively to get somewhere—the banks, customers, tenants, courts, insurance agencies, and so on. No one wants to do business with someone who isn't kind.

DON'T LET IT DISTRACT YOU

S O MANY PEOPLE will try and distract you from following through with your plans for your future.

One day I was working on my website, trying to upload pictures. It was not working, and I was struggling. I figured I was going to have to try something different. As quick as I turn my chair, the Internet goes down. I couldn't get it to reconnect. I also felt defeated in the moment. Maybe I wasn't meant to do it. I decided to pick up my pen and write this page in this book for you.

No one or nothing will stop me from getting where I want to be. I could've given up and tried again tomorrow. I decided to keep creating content regardless of what was trying to stop me. I have to be productive. There are too many pieces to real estate and building a brand that you have to work on. Sometimes five things at a time.

I've been in college for eight years going part time. I failed a few classes in the last eight years. If I stopped there and called it quits, I would've been letting the distraction of failure get to me. Just like hearing that first no. It's failure, and it doesn't feel good.

If you came from where I did, you have nothing to lose. So what if I failed a class? Did they tell me I couldn't retake it? Did they tell me I couldn't come back? These are distractions that we don't think about as distractions.

The biggest distraction to most is friends and relationships. If the people around you don't have the same goals, they will distract you from reaching yours.

COMMITMENT

MOST PEOPLE CAN'T commit to a damn thing. Success will not happen overnight. It is safe to put it in a five-to-ten-year plan. It's a slow grind. I have plenty of time. The alternative is to sit at someone else's dreams for forty hours a week for thirty years before they pay you barely enough to die on.

When you compare it with the time you will put in at a job, it's nothing. It's a commitment to yourself. When I didn't have anything but time on my hands, I would think of ways to add value to my future. I might get up and write a page for this book. I might research the local market for opportunities. I might get up and create more content in the form of websites, shirts, marketing videos, researching other investments, other business ideas. I've committed to my success.

I used to commit to all the wrong things. I committed to hanging out, making people respect me, and making sure no one disrespects me.

People commit every day to thirty years at a job. It's a safe commitment for them. I don't think it's so safe. You've committed your whole livelihood to a company that would fire you faster than the hiring process of you was.

A day job is not a safe commitment. They hold your future. They decide if you get more responsibility. They decide whether you get the raise. Even if you last the thirty years in the company, they'll reward you with just enough to keep you alive until you die after sixty-five years.

I wanted more. I committed to more. I want more for my kid. I want them to commit to themselves before they commit to anyone or a company first.

YOU HAVE KIDS?

HAVE YOU EVER heard a woman say something is too hard to do because she has kids? Like, what? Isn't that the exact reason to do it? They should be your motivation. Don't you want to give your children the world?

I had scheduled a photoshoot for my business cards. I was not planning on taking our son to the shoot. We all have things come up. I could've canceled and rescheduled.

I told our baby to put his shoes on and let's go. I went and handled my business with him. I took a few photos with him! It felt exactly how it should. He is the whole reason why I push myself every day to make something happen. It's hard to hear other mothers talk about how they can't accomplish something because they have kids.

I had help most of the time, but just like anyone, shit happens. We are two parents who worked. Something fell apart one day on our schedules, and I had to keep our son at the same time I had a class. I could've skipped one class, and it probably would've been all right and understandable. Instead, I decided to again tell my son to grab his shoes and let's go. I showed up early so I could catch my professor to ask permission to have my son attend class with me this one time. I was there, and I was ready to learn. She was all for it. I didn't again use my kid to get out of being able to make something happen.

I understand kids can't be at every single event, but they can if it doesn't happen all the time. Use your kids to reach your goals and teach them along the way. You limit yourself; you limit them. They do as much as they see. If you don't believe you can do anything while having them, what do they think they can accomplish themselves.?

People don't intentionally teach their kids these lessons. These are the ripple effects of what we choose to do with our own lives.

I WANT THE same thing I want for my own family. I want you to be happy. I want you to be free to choose to do what you want. It would be dream come true if I could impact millions of young people around the world. I know there are kids who grew up worse or better. Either way, they've felt how I have in my life. I want people all around the world to be able to relate to something I've been through or felt. When you figure out people like you can build something for themselves that they didn't think they could before, amazing things happen.I feel our young people have so much potential, but they are stuck in that vicious cycle. They haven't made a plan outside the things they do on a daily basis.

I learned my potential was power. I understood it could be used for good or bad.

Adults have a hard start in real estate sometimes because some of the decisions they or their parents made. They have debts on their credit report holding them back. They may have even started a family early, and it's now hard to get ahead. It's hard to save money when you are maintaining a whole household, but it has been done.

People have been successful in real estate through childhood traumas and everything else that holds the 90 percent of people back. I want to overcome everything I've been through and become successful. I want the same for anyone who can relate to how bad I wanted something bigger for my future. I didn't know what; I just knew it would be big. I want that for the people who can relate to the feeling. You desperately want it.

I want to reach young people before they have to spend years undoing the choices they made early on that set them back for years. I want to reach people who fell into the very same trap negative mind-set I had growing up, people who have spent years correcting choices they've made too. I want to educate people about real estate, credit, how to use that credit, and life itself. I want to help those people living paycheck to paycheck.

People ask me about my logo LivBetter. I chose that because so many of us are just getting by. We have family and friends we enjoy. We have a car, a job, and a house. Done. At least that's where most of us stop. I don't want people to live good; I want them to LivBetter!

Why wouldn't we want to leave something for our children? What about their children? What about leaving your name behind for your family to remember you, generation after generation? What about setting up a family legacy where generations after you never have to worry about money? What about leaving generations after you content to keep the investments going?

Many people want to tell you money is evil. Money is bad. In the wrong hands, I would agree. I'm talking about me and you. Don't you trust yourself? What about all the people around the world your family could help if you were wealthy? The homeless? The hungry?

I want to teach our children the good it can do. I want them to know money is good, and we can do good things with it.

LIVIA WORLEY

HARD WORK DOESN'T GO UNNOTICED

HAVE YOU FELT like why bother, no one cares? Do you ever feel like you're the only one who cares about you?

I've been working on my bachelor's in business administration at Western Michigan University for eight years. I had a son at eighteen years old and worked two part-time jobs. I made sure to knock a couple of classes a semester down for years to get the point where I can call myself a senior and finally graduate. I graduated in April 2020.

Before I could get to this point, I had exhausted all my financial aid. I could no longer borrow any money to help pay for the rest of my courses a year ago. I was going to have to figure out paying for the rest of my degree out of pocket.

Right when I thought I might have wasted all this time, I got an e-mail from the college. I had been chosen to receive a couple of different scholarships to help pay for my courses!

One was for students specifically like me. I was doing good academically. It was just that the Stanford loan said I had enough. I used my financial aid to pay for a place to live. I used my two part-time jobs to keep up with a son, a house, and transportation. This was nothing short of a miracle. Someone noticed my hard work. I felt like someone was watching over me. Someone noticed I was trying to make something better for myself and my family.

Shit falling apart on us at times are going to happen. We build the tolerance to overcome them. We learn to step back and look at our options. I still worry all the time about things. I've learned to keep moving forward. I can't help or stop everything bad that happens to me, but I can choose how I respond to them.

I know what it's like to have nothing. I know what it's like to spend that last dollar out of my pocket. What's the worse that could happen?

I lose it all? I've had nothing before! I've been with zero before! I know how to make it out of that now! I have the blueprint.

You will probably catch more breaks than heartbreaks. I love real estate. I've had some bad days but not more than I've had good. I had to just push through those bad days. I couldn't give myself a break. I had to figure out what my family is going to do next. It's not just me in this world. I can't let things that fall apart and go unnoticed take over my thoughts. I kept thinking about what I need to do to make this work. Do I need to give it up and find something else? Or is this something that I just need to stick with?

SERVICE OR PRODUCT?

I F YOU WANT to make money, you must have something to offer. Will it be a product or a service? I like them both. There isn't any reason not to provide both under your brand or business investment. If you provide a service, plan an exit. Set it up so you don't have to physically be there for it to operate.

Today it's so much easier to start promoting and growing on today's social media platforms. The customers you need are literally at your fingertips. Way back when before my time, we couldn't reach people without a physical storefront they could come to.

People shop online now. We have platforms to reach those shoppers. Someone who has a social media and has a decent following could possibly have an opportunity on their hands. Or maybe you're the company that reaches out to the person with the big following to maybe help promote your clothing brand. Maybe you give them free clothing to wear and promote on their social media.

Today people still think you must sell every single product or service you create. I would suggest giving out as much free content as possible when you're just starting to build a brand. Give a free book or shirt out here and there. Every dollar from your investment won't come back at the same time. Maybe after giving away free content, someone buys.

I have a social media. Find me. Search LivBetter. I plan on using my platform to grow. To grow my brand, grow my network of people, grow my investments, grow my education, find people who add value, I want to add value to other people. The social media platform is easy, no cost marketing. You can also pay social media to show people your product or service through their ad program. You can pay for advertisements on social media.

Growing up, adults around me had services and products to offer that they weren't selling. I didn't know then, but if I were to go back, I would've told them to save up enough money to start their own brand.

My bio mom used to make all kinds of things. She loved to knit blankets, scarves, and hats. She could start selling on a social media platform. She could create an account, put a logo up, create a pay option, and start putting her things up for sale. She could even take it a step further, offer classes. Teach people how to knit themselves. A product and a service. Charge per person or by the hour.

If financial freedom, the freedom to chose to do what we want is what we are after, we need to figure out the product or service we are trying to sell and build our brand or investment around that.

COVID-19 IN 2020

S INGLEHANDEDLY, EASILY THE biggest news in my book is COVID-19. COVID 19 started to affect American lives in March 2020. For those who live under a rock, COVID-19, or also known as coronavirus, had a human outbreak that originated in China in December 2019.

Our government began to take action in March 2020. They started with restricted airplane travel from certain countries.This specific virus attacks human respiratory system. It was scary because data coming in was hard to use to predict the future. It just seemed people in China were getting sick and dying at an alarming rate.

We had this kind of scare back in 2008 with the swine flu, H1N1. You might remember the 2008 housing market crash, along with the plunging of oil prices. This time the government chose a much more aggressive response. The USA federal government had ordered the shutting down of states and communities, telling people to stay home. Michigan's governor started with shutting down the inside of bars and restaurants, letting them continue with takeout and delivery. She also prohibited large gatherings. It was right before St. Patrick's Day in a college town when they had their work cut out for them. They shut down and blocked off streets. They only let people who live on the street move freely within their street. It felt a lot like martial law.

The idea was not to try and stop the virus but to help slow it down and save lives.

I was in my last few weeks of college when they chose to stop in-person classes and lectures. They had us move to receiving instruction online and remotely from home.

They canceled and postponed my April 2020 graduation ceremony. I was upset at first. All I could think about was how hard I worked to get here. How many years did I sacrifice to get here? I took a lot of time away from my brand and investing in my dreams. I took a ton of time away from my family. For what reward?

After my initial disappointment, I could accept that there is a world crisis more important than a college graduation happening right now. People were losing their lives.

Michigan eventually put a stay-at-home order in place, an order requesting residents to stay in their home. They should only come out for essentials. Businesses that are not essential were requested to close. Grocery stores, gas stations, banks, and public and county professionals were all considered essential.

There were lots of confusion as to who was considered essential and who wasn't. Should fast food be ordered to close? Are they essential? So many people had lost their job by this time. A history-breaking number of unemployment claims after just a couple of weeks of the pandemic. The stock market took a huge hit but not as big as it should have yet. My guess is because people really can't figure out what our economy is going to look like after it's all over.

Many people I talked to from investors to bankers, to realtors, they all say the same thing. They are all very hopeful people will get back to work and that we will bounce back fast.

I don't agree. I do think we will bounce back; I just don't think it will be fast. They will lift the stay-at-home order, but people will still be scared to come out. They won't come out to spend their money with those same crowded locations we were just told to stay away from. It will also take time for those business to recover from the losses they took. They can't just hire the same amount of staff they let go of. With what money? The money they have been banking in during the stay-at-home order. They don't have any sales during any of these months to support that.

The government couldn't give enough money away to help these companies. They did try and make some funding and grants available to some of these businesses. It wasn't enough. They couldn't print off enough money fast enough to help some of these companies. They were dead before the pandemic even started. Most couldn't get their hands on

     LIVIA WORLEY

any help. Too many companies applying for funding that it just wasn't enough to go around to begin with.

Most people don't have $500 in their savings account for a rainy day. These same people go buy companies. They don't get better at managing money. The commercial real estate will probably be the first to collapse or take the biggest hit. How many bars and restaurants can still pay their monthly bills? Even if they can and do, for how long? They don't have any or very little sales coming in.

The airlines were giving out $40 tickets to get from Michigan to Florida, across the country. How long can they last flying an airplane across country for $40? How much money did they lose on that flight?

I just think there hasn't been enough time that went by to see what this country shutdown has done to our economy nationally and locally.

As a landlord during it all, I am making it out okay so far. I only had one tenant say their income was affected. They've paid half the rent, and I said we'd work out the rest. The government is trying to get money out to the people in the way of a one-time, lump-sum payment of $1,200 per adult and $500 per child. They are also giving individuals who claim unemployment because of COVID-19 an additional $600 a week on top of their approved weekly benefit. I'm positive my tenant will take advantage and make it through to stay.

There are other tenants of other landlords who have said they were planning on withholding rent from their landlord. The news coverage, social media, and word of mouth have been spreading about an overwhelming support for tenants to withhold rent, no matter what.

Local courthouses are closed. We couldn't take people to court to evict them for a good reason if we needed to.

That doesn't mean much to me. I wouldn't advise anyone to withhold their rent. Will the courthouses stay closed forever? Has a tenant ever been able to stay anywhere for free for very long? As soon as the courthouse opens is as soon as landlords file their paperwork to evict. After that, tenants have a couple of months, top. Then they're homeless for what reason? Nonpayment of rent. It's one thing to fall behind because a tenant lost their job during the COVID-19 pandemic; it's another thing to have the cash and not pay.

Just plain bad advice. I wouldn't give that advice to my grandmother. It has nothing to do with being a landlord. Common sense tells you no one will let you stay anywhere for very long for free.

The government has tried to offset some of these expenses, but I don't think it will be enough. They gave people like me $1,000 per employee up to $10,000. Maybe enough for some to just stay afloat in the meantime, but I'm not looking to stay afloat. I have money for this rainy day. I'm looking for an opportunity to grow during this pandemic. I am hoping for enough funds to make another investment. I will have to keep my eyes open for more opportunities that come around for investors.

I know commercial real estate like those four-hundred-unit apartment complexes were hit hard. I heard on the news some reported rent payments being down from 30 to 40 percent!

I would hate to be overleveraged through the bank right now. It's important to be smart with your credit. When you have no capital to start, you will go to the bank and use your credit to get something. Don't max out to the point where a public health disaster that no one can predict coming come through and wipe out everything. Be sure to pay things down along the way and give yourself plenty of margin. Never spend your profits. Save them to reinvest them. Have some for a rainy day or rainy months like COVID-19.

AUCTION HOUSE

THERE'S A TAX sale auction that goes on every year during September in my local housing market. These auctions are another opportunity other than bank financing to obtain a property if you don't have a lot of funds. My same rules still apply at auction. I only want move-in ready homes or homes that have low repair costs to bring it to move-in ready.

This is difficult to find in these auctions because of the limited information that's given out. They don't give out any good photos and definitely not of the inside of these properties. We call it site unseen. Lots of the houses in my local market aren't in great condition, much less good condition.

We choose to do research. Strict rules prohibit the public from going to any of the properties listed. These houses are in this specific type of auction because the owners are back on taxes and owe. Some are disgruntled. For safety reasons, they ask you don't go knocking on doors, but we will drive by and see in person the condition of the property. We want to see the condition of the neighbor's house and the condition of the neighborhood as a whole. I will call local townships or city buildings to see if there were any recent inspections and the notes from the inspector. I'll check the last time the house sold, when and for how much.

I want occupied homes in the tax sale auction. Most of the public investors in my local market are scared of occupied properties. I'm not. I know the eviction process isn't scary. It puts me at an advantage over other people at these auctions.

My theory on occupied houses are they have to be in somewhat decent condition inside that people are living in it currently. Yes, people can live in terrible conditions, but that's the risk associated with site unseen.

I always make sure to save enough money to buy a property at auction plus some for the work I will put in to make it move-in ready. At least $5,000 to be sure. The money I have to buy the house plus any repairs and the knowledge about the eviction process make for little competition at the tax sale auctions every year.

The price to purchase these homes has risen each year. A house bought at auction in 2012 to 2013 was only $4,500 to $6,000. At last year's tax sale auction in 2019, there wasn't a house that went for less than $30,000.

I got one in the 2017 tax sale auction for about $15,000. That's our max for any house bought at auction. I put about $5,000 after purchase for repairs. I was able to rent it out for first month's rent and deposit in November, about three months after purchase. The eviction process was two2 months. Repairs, listing and showing the property, and picking a qualified tenant were about a month.

I also think this year's tax sale auction will give me a good first look into what the COVID-19 public health crisis did to our local housing market and investors. What will be the impact on prices at the tax sale auction?

CONSULTATIONS AND MOTIVATIONAL SPEAKING

I'M IN THE first few stages of building my brand. Right now, I'm building a platform to be able to host motivational speaking nights and content videos. I want to upload content about life, experiences I went through growing up, and my journey investing in real estate. I want to provide people with my experience overcoming barriers. I'm working on a podcast right now called 6–11 podcast. The idea is that most people work a 9–5 job, and so they have 6–11 they can work on their dreams.

I'm putting together material for viewers who want to start working toward saving to invest in their dreams. I want to give people content of everyday struggles and being able to arise above them.

I want to put energy in the world that's unbreakable. I want to build a network of family that overtakes the industry. We should be learning from one another.

I have a voice I want to share with the world. There's someone out there who needs to hear my message. I want to help them.

LivBetter is a consultation service I provide. I consult about investment practices, building brands, living your dreams. Anyone can find me on LinkedIn, Facebook, or Instagram. Just search Liv Better. Come check me out online and join the LivBetter family!

RECAP ZERO TO HUNDREDS OF THOUSANDS IN REAL ESTATE

F OR THOSE WHO want a small recap of how I went from zero to hundreds of thousands in real estate, I started with nothing. I grew poor. I never had what I saw other kids with that I wanted. When I had to constantly think about how we don't have enough for something or we have to go without, it built a hunger in me for success. Once I was able to channel it properly as a young adult, I was able to gain traction.

I found a job and got stable. Once I was stable, I was so disciplined about how I spent my money. I never spent it. I saved it. I saved enough to use the bank as leverage to buy my first few properties. I added value and refinanced them for more money. I used the money to buy more real estate. I used every rent dollar made to go back into more real estate. I used rent money to buy another property. By the time I looked up, I had hundreds of thousands in real estate and graduated with my bachelor's in accounting—crazy!

I know with the right set of skills, the financial competence, and a team of reliable experts, anyone can do it.

GET ACTIVATED. GET motivated. You have to really want this shit. We don't have anything to lose when you came from the bottom. Jump into what you want to do. You won't learn everything you need to by research. Most of it you will learn along the way as you run into them. I usually don't know what's going on, and I'm knee-deep in it.

I'm definitely guilty of this. I want everything to be perfect. It's not, and it won't be. We have to find the middle ground that says okay, let's put it out there and see what people think.

Imagine spending five years on creating the perfect product, doing all the research you could, building out of the best quality materials to hit the market running, but no one cares about the end product, or maybe there is a better cheaper one out already because someone else didn't think they needed as much time to create what people wanted. You're late. Too much research. Take action!

Create something within three months. After reading this book, come find me on social media and share your story. When I say create something, I mean a product or service. If you're building a brand or growing a company that can take years to be as successful as you want it, that takes time and dedication.

It's okay. Three months isn't that long, but we have it easier today. We Google everything. Even if we can't find, let's say, an expert in designing websites. Those are hard, but we have the option of researching ourselves and learning at a much faster rate.Can you solve problems? Do you always look for solutions? Are you always helping someone else with their problems? You're a natural entrepreneur! You will create something people want.

I'M GRATEFUL I will have a lot of people support me. I'll have family, friends, people I've touched along the way, and people who just plain out support the vision I have. My sister has been one of the longest lasting supporters I have in my life, from beginning to start. I'm grateful to have spent many years with her and enjoy so many things in our childhood despite what we've seen. We enjoyed playing outside, riding bikes, playing basketball, swimming, and sticking together in school. We had different likes and interests but always seemed to find something to do together. I'm thankful to have the good memories I do have from growing up with her. I wouldn't want to do any of that growing up with anyone else!

I assume people are interested in how I got here, what it took in me to change some of the decisions I was making when I was younger because of what I've been through.

I bet anyone who knew me then would've never guessed where I am today and how far I've came. I was one of the worst kids who went through Berrien County in Michigan. They didn't think there was a chance in hell I'd do something good. I was in residential because of my own actions. I might not have been able to change the environment I grew up in, but I can change how respond to things now. I have that power. We have to show one another the power we hold over our own lives. We have to see that we have control over our future. We are only under someone else's roof for so long, and even worse, we will just end up under someone else's roof from 9–5 p.m. if we don't acknowledge the power we hold.

We have to be kind to one another. People who have touched me in my life are some of the same people reading this book, people who showed kindness to me when they didn't have to. They weren't getting anything in return. Those people showed me how much kindness matters.

Be kind to the members of society that no one else is. I was expelled from my high school by grade 9, on my way down the school to prison pipeline, locked up at fifteen, had two intensive probation officers in two different counties, and had at least been charged with ten crimes by age fifteen. These are people who desperately need kindness. People were kind to me when I wasn't kind to them. Those people shaped me into who I am today.

I want you to spread the word. Reach out to people with my story, people you know could relate, someone who could be helped by reading this. I want them to know how to guide and structure themselves for success. I want to reach as many as those people as possible. Spread the word to anyone you know who may need a mentor or coach. Spread it to someone who is working a day job and wants to get out.Last, I want to thank you. Thank you for supporting me. I want to thank people who supported me along the way and never gave up on me! I also want to thank you in supporting yourself. You want something better, or you know someone who does. You took a step in toward figuring out what's next for you, and hopefully, I left you with plenty to think about.

ABOUT THE AUTHOR

LIVIA GREW UP very poor and built a "trust no one" mentality after enduring a rough childhood that led her down a road of criminal charges and locked up at age fifteen. Upon release, she dropped out of high school and had a baby at age eighteen. Having a son and changing the way she viewed life created a fire to go back to school, find a day job, and save enough money by changing the way she thought about money and eliminating unnecessary spending to invest in houses, producing hundreds of thousands in real estate.